THE WILD WEST

THE TRANSCONTINENTAL RAILROAD

by Christine Zuchora-Walske

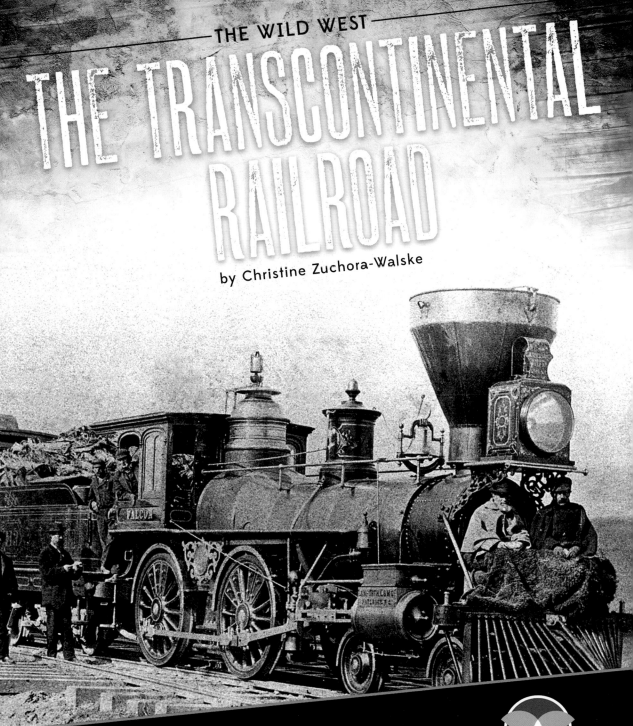

Content Consultant
Dr. Gregory Schneider
Professor of History
Emporia State University

Core Library

An Imprint of Abdo Publishing
abdopublishing.com

abdopublishing.com

Published by Abdo Publishing, a division of ABDO, PO Box 398166, Minneapolis, Minnesota 55439. Copyright © 2017 by Abdo Consulting Group, Inc. International copyrights reserved in all countries. No part of this book may be reproduced in any form without written permission from the publisher. Core Library™ is a trademark and logo of Abdo Publishing.

Printed in the United States of America, North Mankato, Minnesota
042016
092016

Cover Photo: AP Images
Interior Photos: AP Images, 1; GraphicaArtis/Corbis, 4; JLBeuzon 1933/PVDE/Bridgeman Images, 6; North Wind Picture Archives, 8, 19; Picture History/Newscom, 12; Carleton E. Watkins, 15; Red Line Editorial, 21, 39; Corbis, 24, 26, 45; Tarker/Corbis, 30; Underwood Archives/UIG Universal Images Group/Newscom, 34; Hulton-Deutsch Collection/Corbis, 36; Alessia Pierdomenico/Bloomberg via Getty Images, 40

Editor: Claire Mathiowetz
Series Designer: Ryan Gale

Cataloging-in-Publication Data
Names: Zuchora-Walske, Christine, author.
Title: The Transcontinental Railroad / by Christine Zuchora-Walske.
Description: Minneapolis, MN : Abdo Publishing, [2017] | Series: The wild West
    | Includes bibliographical references and index.
Identifiers: LCCN 2015960509 | ISBN 9781680782615 (lib. bdg.) |
    ISBN 9781680776720 (ebook)
Subjects: LCSH: Pacific railroads--History--Juvenile literature. | Railroads--
    United States--History--Juvenile literature. | Frontier and pioneer life ((U.S.)--
    Juvenile literature.
Classification: DDC 385.0973--dc23
LC record available at http://lccn.loc.gov/2015960509

CONTENTS

THE ROAD TO THE RAILROAD

In the late 1700s, the British ruled 13 North American colonies. When the American Revolutionary War (1775–1783) ended, the colonies became the United States of America. This sparked the beginning of a transformative period for the United States. The new country stretched from the Mississippi River to the Atlantic Ocean. It reached from the Great Lakes almost to the Gulf of Mexico.

The Louisiana Purchase included 827,000 square miles (2.14 million sq km) of land.

Columbus landing in the Americas with the Spanish flag in 1492

In just a short time, the United States doubled in size. In 1803 the United States bought a big chunk of land from France. France had claimed the plains between the Rocky Mountains and the Mississippi River. But now the United States owned that land. The deal was called the Louisiana Purchase. By 1848 the country spread all the way from the Pacific Ocean to the Atlantic Ocean.

The Changing Face of North America

However, North America was not empty when Europeans first arrived. In 1492 Christopher Columbus landed in the Americas. North America was already home to millions of people. They had lived there for thousands of years. These people became known as Native Americans. But actually they belonged to hundreds of different nations.

As the border of the United States crept westward, white settlers followed. Some of the first white people who moved west of the Mississippi were fur trappers and traders. Other westward travelers wanted land for farming and raising animals. Some white settlers thought it was their religious duty to move west. This belief was part of an idea known as the Manifest Destiny.

In 1848 gold was discovered in California. After that discovery, many more people moved west hoping to get rich.

Fights sometimes broke out between Native Americans and white settlers.

As white people moved to the West, they met the Native Americans who lived there. Sometimes these meetings were friendly. But often the interactions were angry—or even deadly. Tensions were rising. White people were taking control of Native American lands. The Native American population was quickly decreasing because of the settlers. The face of North America was changing.

A Hard Journey

During the early and mid-1800s, people could travel from the East to the West in two ways. Both were long, dangerous, and uncomfortable.

One method was by sea. A traveler could sail on a ship down around South America. That journey took about six weeks. The sea could be dangerous, especially at the southern tip of South America. Seasickness and cramped quarters made the trip miserable. Some people sailed to Central America instead. They got off the ship and crossed Central America to the Pacific Ocean. Then they got on another ship and sailed north. Crossing on land saved time and avoided the perils of the southern sea. But people faced the danger of tropical diseases in the Central American rain forests.

Another way to travel to the West was by horse-drawn wagon. This took about six months. It meant trudging across grasslands and deserts and over rivers and mountains. People traveled through rain and snow. They lived outdoors for months. It also meant facing Native Americans, who might attack the travelers, seeing them as intruders.

Manifest Destiny

Manifest Destiny was an American belief in the early 1800s. This idea said that the United States was the best country that had ever existed. It also said that the United States had to set an example for the rest of the world. People believed it was their duty to make the nation stretch all the way from the Atlantic to the Pacific. They believed this was God's plan. They also thought that the future of America depended on it. People believed prosperity waited for those who journeyed west.

A Better Way

The journey across the United States was so hard that the East and West were almost disconnected. It was difficult to visit loved ones, ship goods, and share ideas. Many people longed for a better way to travel, trade, and communicate.

Americans began building railroads along the East Coast in 1828. Soon people began to dream of a railroad crossing the entire continent. It would be a huge task. But the dreamers were determined to get it done.

EXPLORE ONLINE

Chapter One explains why many Americans wanted a coast-to-coast railroad. The website below offers a glimpse of what a wagon trip to the West was like for kids. How is the information from the website the same as the information in Chapter One? What new information did you learn from the website?

Kids on the Trail

mycorelibrary.com/transcontinental-railroad

CHAPTER TWO

THE CENTRAL PACIFIC RAILROAD

The United States' first railroads began running in approximately 1830. At first they were short lines. The very first one, called the Baltimore & Ohio (B&O) Railroad, ran only 13 miles (21 km). But almost immediately, Americans began talking about longer tracks. Some even started dreaming of a coast-to-coast railroad.

An early version of a Baltimore & Ohio Railroad locomotive

Early Dreamers

Over the next decade, some Americans offered the idea of a transcontinental railroad. But few people took them seriously. Then Asa Whitney came along. Whitney thought a transcontinental railroad was the best way to connect Americans. It could ease trade, travel, and communication.

In 1845 Whitney proposed the plan for a transcontinental railroad to Congress. He gave speeches and visited local leaders. He wrote letters to newspapers.

But many Americans thought Whitney's railroad was impossibly long. The northern climate was too harsh. The Native Americans along the route were too dangerous. Many Southerners thought the northern route was unfair because it did not serve the South at all.

In 1851 Whitney gave up. Even though he did not reach his goal, he inspired people to talk about railroads.

Theodore Judah studied civil engineering when he was a student.

"Crazy Judah"

In the early 1850s, American attitudes toward a transcontinental railroad began to change. California became a state. People were streaming there in search of land and gold. In 1853 Congress sent surveyors to study and measure the western land. They looked for possible railroad routes to California.

In 1854 a young man named Theodore Judah moved to California. Judah was a railroad surveyor.

His job was to build a short line through the Sacramento Valley. It was the first railroad west of the Missouri River.

Judah finished this job in 1856. Then he tackled his real dream: helping build a transcontinental railroad. He was so excited about this transcontinental line that some people called him "Crazy Judah." He could talk for hours about railroads.

Judah knew a coast-to-coast railroad was a huge, tricky job. First he needed to find a route. The route had to go either around or through the Sierra Nevada. It was the mountain range covering eastern California. Then he had to figure out the cost of workers, supplies, and equipment. Those workers would need to level land, lay rails, build bridges, and blast tunnels. To solve these puzzles, Judah had to survey California.

In 1860 a local storekeeper told Judah about a possible route through the Sierra Nevada. Judah convinced four California businessmen to pay for a survey of this route. He did the survey and drew up maps.

In 1861 he went to Washington, DC. He showed his maps to lawmakers. Many thought the project was too expensive. But others were interested. They proposed a bill allowing the US government to pay for the railroad. In 1862 Congress passed the bill. President Abraham Lincoln signed it into law.

The law was named the Pacific Railway Act. It gave Judah's company, the Central

PERSPECTIVES
"We Were Making Money"

This quote comes from a 1903 article written by a Chinese American immigrant who provided laundry services for the CPRR workers:

When I first opened a laundry it was in company with a partner . . . where a railroad was building. Our rent cost us $10 a month and food nearly $5 a week each. . . . It cost us about $50 for our furniture and apparatus, and we made close upon $60 a week, which we divided between us. We had to put up with many insults and some frauds. . . . On the other hand, we were making money, and even after sending home $3 a week I was able to save about $15. . . .

Pacific Railroad (CPRR), the right to build eastward from Sacramento, California. The law also created a second company. It was called the Union Pacific Railroad (UPRR). The UPRR would build a railway westward from the Missouri River. The act promised the companies 6,400 acres (2,590 ha) of land. It also promised up to $48,000 for each mile (1.6 km) of track they built.

Building Eastward

The CPRR broke ground in January 1863. The company's biggest challenge was the land itself. The Sierra Nevada is a steep and rocky mountain range. The mountains are littered with boulders, cut by rivers, and dotted with soaring cliffs.

Workers had to build a bridge across every river and valley. They cut trees from the mountains to make wooden frames. They put those frames together to make tall, skinny trestles, or raised railways.

In some places, the workers had to chisel into steep mountainsides to make ledges wide enough

Chinese workers taking a break from building a railroad

for a train. One mountain called Cape Horn towered nearly 1,300 feet (400 m) over a river. The railway ledge around Cape Horn was built during the winter of 1865–1866. It was 1,500 feet (460 m) long.

Sometimes the CPRR's track had to go through mountains. Workers blasted 15 tunnels through solid rock. One of these, the Summit Tunnel, was approximately 1,700 feet (520 m) long. To make the tunnel, groups of men worked in eight-hour shifts around the clock. They drilled holes in the rock. The men packed the holes with explosive black powder. They attached fuses, lit them, and fled the tunnels quickly. This hard, dangerous work dug about 1 foot (0.3 m) of tunnel per day. Then a stronger explosive called dynamite became available. The amount dug per day doubled. Digging this tunnel took from August 1866 to November 1867.

Nature offered another challenge too. The weather in the mountains was terrible. Snowstorms raged all winter. The brutal winter of 1866–1867 brought 44 snowstorms. One storm dropped 6 feet (2 m) of snow. It was too much to clear. Avalanches were destroying trestles and killing workers. So in summer 1867, the CPRR began building snow sheds. These were long, wooden, tunnel-like sheds with roofs sloping over the tracks. From 1867 to 1869, CPRR workers built 37 miles (60 km) of snow sheds.

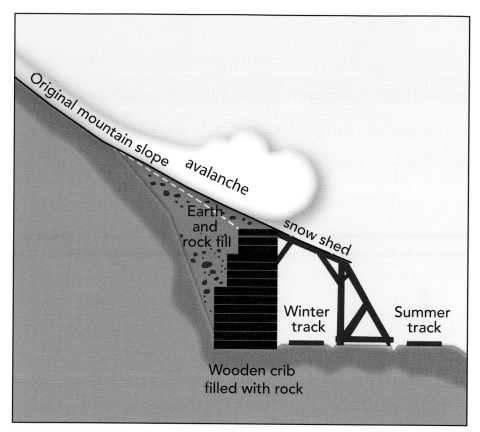

Original mountain slope

avalanche

Earth and rock fill

snow shed

Winter track

Summer track

Wooden crib filled with rock

How a Snow Shed Works

This diagram shows how a snow shed protects a railroad track from heavy mountain snowfalls and avalanches. Take a look at the diagram. Why do you think railroad workers needed to build the wooden crib filled with rock into the snow shed?

The Central Pacific Workforce

The CPRR easily laid track between Sacramento and the Sierra Nevada. But the company could not find enough workers for the mountain route. Most of the men wanted to stay near the towns, where life was easier. Others wanted to be near the gold and silver mines, where they might get rich.

California was home to many Chinese immigrants who were looking for work. The CPRR bosses believed Chinese men were too small and weak for railroad work. Finally though, the company hired them.

From Guangdong to California

Large numbers of Chinese people began moving to the United States in 1850. Most came from Guangdong province in southeastern China. Conditions there were bad after decades of famine, floods, and war. Many Chinese men crossed the Pacific Ocean to find work, start businesses, or strike it rich.

The Chinese laborers were excellent workers, despite getting paid less than whites and facing constant discrimination. The company started recruiting Chinese immigrants all over California and even in China. By 1868 the CPRR's workforce was 80 percent Chinese.

Thanks largely to these Chinese workers, the CPRR finally made it over the mountains and into Nevada in May 1868. Now the race was on. The company wanted to lay track swiftly. It wanted to claim as many miles as possible before meeting up with the UPRR somewhere in Utah.

FURTHER EVIDENCE

Reread this chapter. Find its main point. List the key evidence you see to support that point. Then read the article from the link below. Find a quote in the article that supports the chapter's main point. Does the quote support a piece of evidence you found in the chapter or add a new one?

Rails to the Pacific

mycorelibrary.com/transcontinental-railroad

CHAPTER THREE

THE UNION PACIFIC RAILROAD

Nature was not a problem for the Union Pacific Railroad. The Union Pacific's biggest problem was people.

Cheater in Charge

Thomas C. Durant was in charge of the westward construction of the Union Pacific. Durant was eager to build a railroad. But he did not believe it could make money by carrying passengers and cargo. Durant did

Thomas C. Durant was also the founder of the Missouri & Mississippi Railroad.

A group of men building the Union Pacific Railroad through Nebraska

not care whether the railroad succeeded or failed. He just wanted to be in charge of building it. That way he could get his hands on the payments from the US government.

In December 1863, the Union Pacific broke ground in Omaha, Nebraska. It was supposed to start across the Missouri River in Council Bluffs, Iowa. But Durant put off building a difficult, expensive bridge. He owned land in Omaha. His property would be more valuable if the railroad started there. Eastern lines from Chicago, Illinois, were also being built to connect with the railroad in Omaha. Workers started building the roadbed through eastern Nebraska in March 1864. In July they laid the first rail.

Meanwhile surveyors found a route through Nebraska and Wyoming to Utah. In November 1864, President Lincoln approved the route. In December Durant made the route 9 miles (14 km) longer. He said the new route was less steep. But that was not the real reason. Durant could make more money and buy more acres alongside the railroad with a longer route.

Durant had other tricks up his sleeve too. In 1864 he formed a company called Credit Mobilier. Through this company, Durant and a few handpicked partners quietly controlled a construction company. The company's owner was Durant's friend. Durant paid him to charge much more than the railroad construction actually cost. Then he directed the money straight to Credit Mobilier. Even some members of Congress participated in the scam and profited greatly.

Durant's cheating bothered Peter Dey, the UPRR's chief engineer. Dey was an honest man. He could not stand working for a dishonest one. He quit in 1865.

Despite Durant's scheming and Dey's quitting, the Union Pacific did manage to build a bit of the railroad. By the end of 1865, it had 40 miles (64 km) of track.

A Rough Life

Many UPRR workers were Civil War veterans. Life was unpleasant for them. Their quarters were crowded and uncomfortable. Most of the men had lice. There was little chance to bathe. Their food included beef, hard bread, boiled beans, and black coffee. Their water often contained harmful bacteria, so diarrhea was a big problem. The railroad camp had a horrible stench.

"Hell on Wheels"

In 1865 government officials began to lose faith in the UPRR. The company was not getting much done. Members of the government started talking about cutting off funding. Durant did not want to lose this money-making opportunity. So he got to work.

In 1866 Durant hired Grenville Dodge to take Dey's place as chief engineer. Dodge hired Jack Casement to manage construction. Dodge and Casement had no problem with Durant's cheating. Casement found workers easily. The US Civil War (1861–1865) had recently ended. Thousands of soldiers needed jobs. So did thousands of Irish immigrants.

Union Pacific construction finally picked up some speed. By summer 1866, it was laying 2 to 3 miles

PERSPECTIVES
Letters from Home

Many railroad workers left families at home, missing them. This quote comes from a letter written by Frances Casement to her husband on December 11, 1866.

> Our boy is growing finely. . . . If you don't come home & Stay with us some this winter you will never know any thing more of this baby than you did of your first. . . . I am thinking of you all the time. . . . I do love you darling more than I can tell and hope before long you will be at home with us and we shall have a happy time. . . .
> Your loving Wife
> Frank

Native Americans attacking a UPRR train

(3 to 5 km) of track a day. As the railroad stretched steadily west, the workers followed. They slept in tents or train cars. The workers built a station every 100 miles (161 km). As stations sprang up, so did towns. The towns offered shops, saloons, dance halls, gambling houses, and every business that rough working men might want. The towns were so wild that a newspaper editor dubbed the towns "Hell on Wheels."

Native American Lands

Not all UPRR workers worried about the bosses' cheating or the hard work. But many worried about the dangers of intruding on Native American lands.

White settlers had been pushing westward for decades. Their numbers kept growing. The railroad began creeping across the plains. Native Americans could see that white people meant to take over the land.

White settlers were killing off the bison herds that the Native Americans depended on to survive.

Sometimes settlers attacked the Native Americans. Many Native Americans had to move off their ancestral lands. Some Native Americans fought back by stealing from or attacking the intruders.

Many whites felt Native Americans were dangerous. They feared that towns and travelers would never be safe until the Native Americans were gone. Many Native Americans felt similarly toward white people. Native Americans knew they were outnumbered. But they hoped to keep some of their land and their way of life. So groups of Cheyenne, Sioux, and Arapaho constantly harassed the Union Pacific workers. They pulled up surveyors' stakes, cut telegraph wires, tore up tracks, and derailed trains. They shot and killed workers with arrows and bullets.

But these attacks did not stop Durant, Dodge, and Casement. The Union Pacific Railroad marched on through western Nebraska and southern Wyoming. Soon it entered Utah.

In the book *The Fighting Cheyennes*, a young Cheyenne named Porcupine describes seeing train tracks for the first time in 1915:

We saw the first train of cars that any of us had seen. We looked at it from a high ridge. Far off it was very small, but it kept coming and growing larger all the time, puffing out smoke and steam, and as it came on we said to each other that it looked like a white man's pipe when he was smoking. . . . As we talked of our troubles, we said among ourselves: "Now the white people have taken all we had and have made us poor and we ought to do something. In these big wagons that go on this metal road, there must be things that are valuable. . . . If we could throw these wagons off the iron they run on and break them open, we should find out what was in them and could take whatever might be useful to us."

Source: George Bird Grinnell. The Fighting Cheyennes. *Norman, OK: University of Oklahoma Press, 1983. Print. 256–257.*

Changing Minds

This quote gives an example of a Native American attack on UPRR workers. Take a position on this conflict. Then imagine your best friend has the opposite opinion. Write a short essay trying to change your friend's mind. Detail your reasons. Include facts that support your reasons.

CHAPTER FOUR

PROMONTORY SUMMIT AND BEYOND

By March 1869, the CPRR and UPRR had both reached northern Utah. Both companies wanted to lay as much track as possible. More track meant more land and money. Neither wanted to stop building. Both groups refused to identify a meeting point for their tracks.

President Ulysses S. Grant called the company bosses to Washington, DC. He said if they could not

The celebration of the two railroads when they met at Promontory Summit on April 10, 1869

The late 1800s sparked a boom in railroad construction all over the continent.

agree on a meeting place, the government would choose one. The bosses argued for days. Finally, on April 10, they announced that the tracks would meet at Promontory Summit. It was located north of Utah's Great Salt Lake.

The Last Spike

On May 10, the Central Pacific and Union Pacific locomotives met nose to nose. Before a large crowd, the bosses of both companies each drove in a spike to join the railroads.

The hammers clanged at about 12:57 p.m. local time. Telegraph wires were connected to the spikes. The wires sent signals in both directions across the United States.

The crowd erupted with cheers. A band played. Officials gave champagne toasts. The ceremonies continued with photographs, feasting, and music.

The 10-Mile Day

On April 28, 1869, the CPRR built a record-breaking 10 miles (16 km) of track. A crew of 848 workers laid 25,800 wooden ties. Workers drove in 55,000 spikes and laid 3,520 iron rails. The rails were joined with 7,040 fishplates (metal bars that connect two rails on a track). The workers who carried the rails hauled 2 million pounds (910,000 kg) of iron that day!

The Railroad's Legacy

The transcontinental railroad had far-reaching effects on the United States. Its quickest and most dramatic impacts were on transportation, trade, and

Promontory Summit

Army lieutenant J. C. Currier attended the event at Promontory Summit. He wrote about it in his diary:

> *The telegraph wires were so arranged that the taps were flashed to all parts of the US so that eager thousands in all the great cities knew the rail was laid and the R.R. complete. Truly it was worth the trip from New Hampshire alone to see this great achievement. Two beautifully decorated engines, one of each road advanced until the guards touched—the engineers climbed out and broke a bottle of champagne across the space and shook hands.*

communication. The railroad began carrying passengers and cargo immediately. Now people and goods could travel from the East to the West in two weeks instead of six months. The journey would be one-tenth of the old cost. By 1880 the UPRR and CPRR were hauling $50 million worth of freight every year.

The railroad also sped up white settlement of the West. As the trip out West became easier, quicker, and cheaper, more people came. By 1880 settlers were farming more than

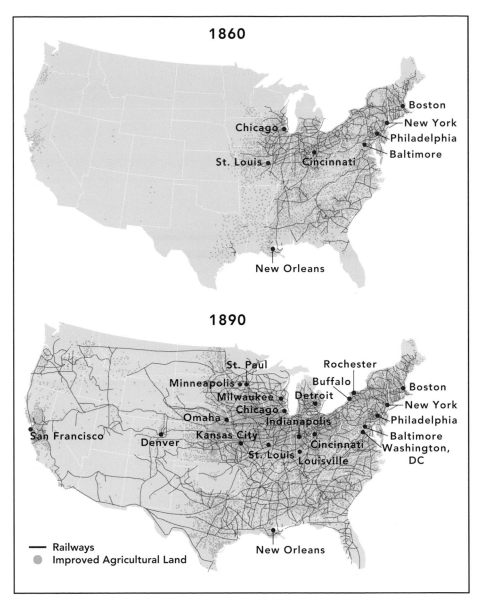

1860

Boston
New York
Chicago
Philadelphia
Baltimore
St. Louis
Cincinnati

New Orleans

1890

St. Paul
Rochester
Minneapolis
Buffalo
Milwaukee
Detroit
Boston
Chicago
Omaha
New York
Indianapolis
Philadelphia
San Francisco
Baltimore
Denver
Kansas City
Cincinnati
Washington,
St. Louis
Louisville
DC

New Orleans

—— Railways
● Improved Agricultural Land

US Growth

The map above shows how US railroads, farms, and cities with a population of more than 100,000 people grew between 1860 and 1890. Compare the two maps. How many more large US cities developed from 1860 to 1890? In what areas of the country did railroads develop the most?

Trains have changed greatly in the last century, but they are still used for transporting goods and people.

2 million acres of what had been Native American land. The bison nearly went extinct. And Native Americans were forced onto reservations far away from the railroad.

In 1890 the US government did a census. It found that Americans had settled the nation's wild spaces. The frontier, officials declared, had disappeared. And the legacy of the railroad continued on into the 1900s.

In his book *Roughing It*, American novelist and journalist Mark Twain wrote about his experience with the railroad:

> *Fifty-six hours out from St. Joe [Missouri]—THREE HUNDRED MILES! Now that was stage-coaching on the great overland, ten or twelve years ago, when perhaps not more than ten men in America, all told, expected to live to see a railroad follow that route to the Pacific. But the railroad is there, now, and it pictures a thousand odd comparisons and contrasts in my mind to read the following sketch . . . of a recent trip over almost the very ground I have been describing. . . . "At 4:20 P.M., Sunday, we rolled out of the station at Omaha, and started westward on our long jaunt. . . . Monday at eight o'clock, [we found] ourselves at the crossing of the North Platte, three hundred miles from Omaha—fifteen hours and forty minutes out."*

Source: Mark Twain. Roughing It. Hartford, CT: American Publishing Company, 1872. Print. 46–47.

Point of View

Read both "Straight to the Source" texts in the book. Think about the two writers' points of view. Write a short essay that answers these questions: What is the point of view of each author? How are they similar and why? How are they different and why?

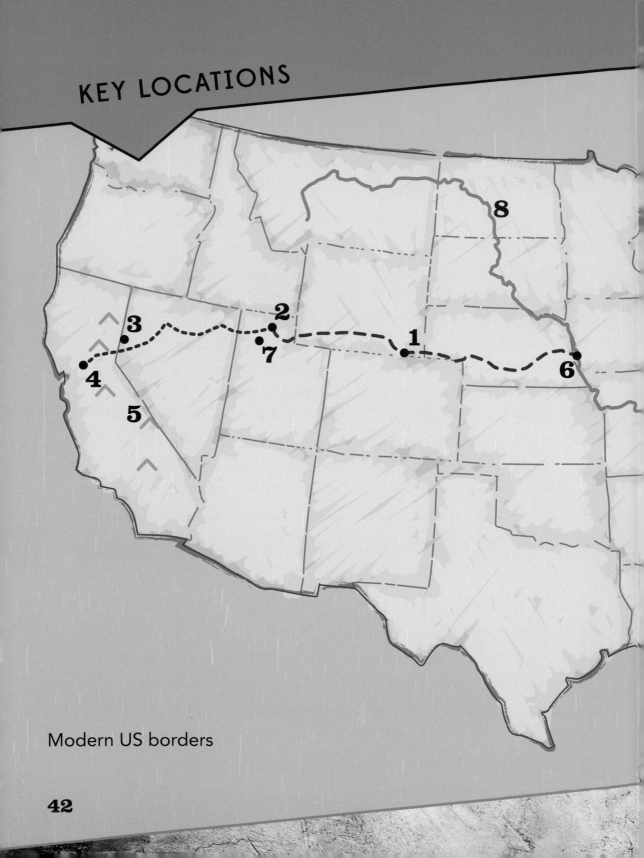

Modern US borders

The Transcontinental Railroad, 1869

•••••• Central Pacific Railroad (Sacramento, California, to Promontory Summit, Utah)

— — — Union Pacific Railroad (Promontory Summit, Utah, to Omaha, Nebraska)

1. Cheyenne, Wyoming

2. Promontory Summit, Utah

3. Reno, Nevada

4. Sacramento, California

5. Sierra Nevada

6. Council Bluffs, Iowa

7. Great Salt Lake

8. Missouri River

STOP AND THINK

Tell the Tale

Chapter One of this book discusses the experiences of Americans traveling to the West before the transcontinental railroad was built. Imagine you are making a similar trip. Write 200 words about the adventures you have, the dangers you encounter, and the hardships you endure.

Say What?

Studying American history can mean learning a lot of new vocabulary. Find five words in this book you have never heard before. Use a dictionary to find out what they mean. Then write the meanings in your own words, and use each word in a new sentence.

Surprise Me

Chapters Two and Three discuss some of the transcontinental railroad workers' challenges and achievements. After reading these chapters, what two facts did you find most surprising? Write a few sentences about each fact. Why did you find each fact surprising?

Dig Deeper

After reading this book, what questions do you still have about the transcontinental railroad? With an adult's help, find a few reliable sources that can help you answer your questions. Write a paragraph about what you learned.

GLOSSARY

engineer
a person who is trained in developing and using nature's power and resources in ways that are useful to people

famine
an extreme shortage of food

locomotive
a train engine that pushes or pulls the cars

Manifest Destiny
the early 1800s American belief that the United States should stretch all the way from the Atlantic to the Pacific

roadbed
the foundation of a railroad; the surface upon which tracks are laid

snow shed
a wooden, tunnel-like shed with a sloping roof built over a railroad track to protect the track from heavy snowfalls and avalanches

survey
to find out the size, shape, and position of the land

telegraph
an electric device or system for sending messages by a code over wires

transcontinental
crossing a whole continent

trestle
a structure made of wood or steel for carrying a railroad over a valley

LEARN MORE

Books

Floca, Brian. *Locomotive.* New York: Atheneum/
Richard Jackson Books, 2014.

Sandler, Martin W. *Iron Rails, Iron Men, and the
Race to Link the Nation.* Somerville, MA:
Candlewick Press, 2015.

Yasuda, Anita. *Westward Expansion of the United
States: 1801–1861.* Minneapolis, MN: Abdo
Publishing, 2014.

Websites

To learn more about the Wild West, visit
booklinks.abdopublishing.com. These links are
routinely monitored and updated to provide the most
current information available.

Visit **mycorelibrary.com** for free additional tools for
teachers and students.

INDEX

ABOUT THE AUTHOR

Christine Zuchora-Walske studied literature, communications, and publishing at the University of Notre Dame and the University of Denver. She has been writing and editing children's books and articles for more than 20 years.